THE YORKSHIRE DALES

John Potter

CONTENTS

MYRIAD
LONDON

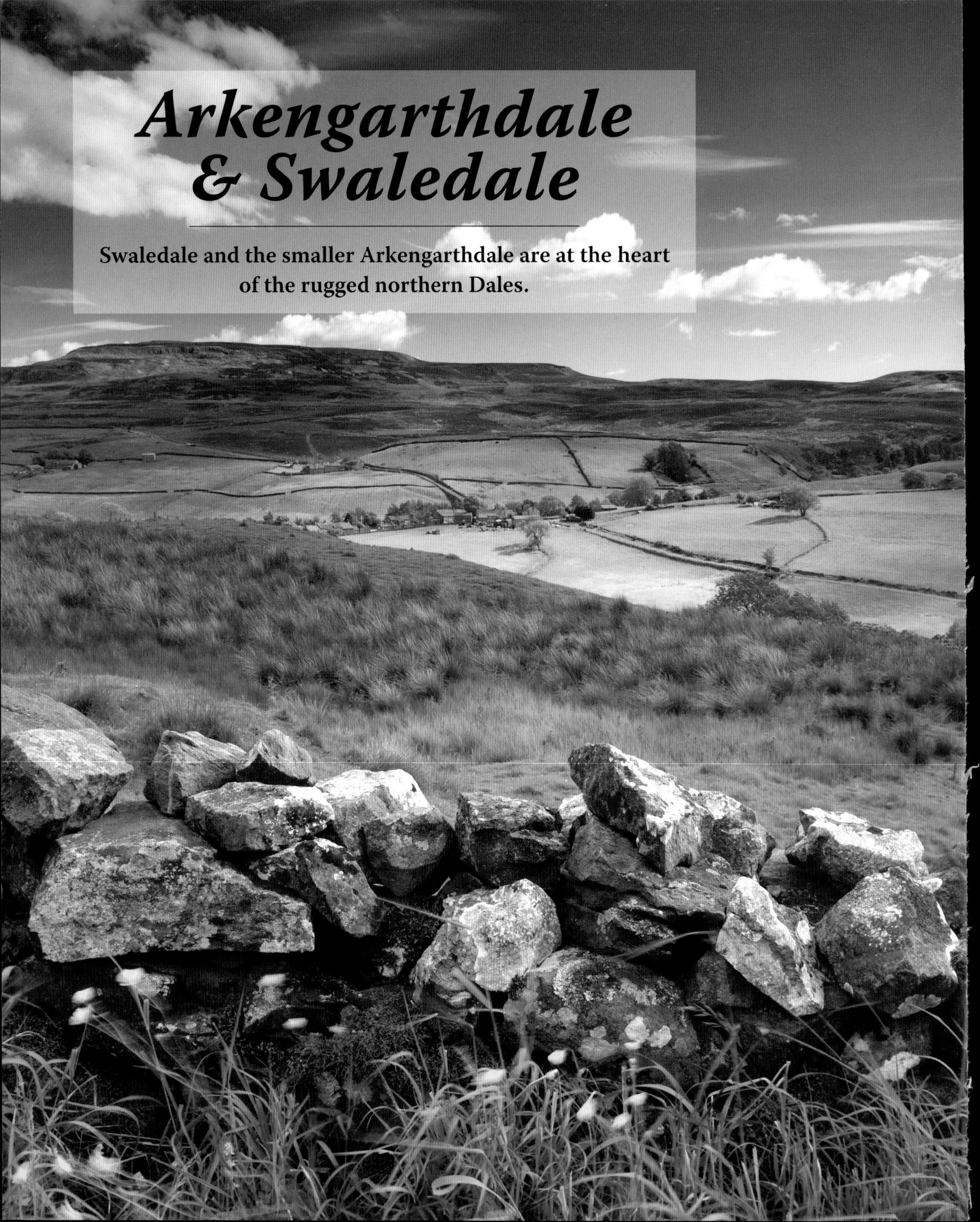

Arkengarthdale & Swaledale

Swaledale and the smaller Arkengarthdale are at the heart of the rugged northern Dales.

Flowing through Swaledale is the river Swale, which rises high up on peat moors to the west in Cumbria. This area contains the upland villages of Keld and Muker, together with Gunnerside, Reeth and Richmond, the capital of Swaledale. Arkengarthdale is a remote, sparsely populated tributary dale which joins Swaledale from the north-west, with Arkle Beck at its heart. This most northerly Dale contains the tiny settlements of Arkle Town and Langthwaite, once the centre of a long-deserted leadmining industry, now a peaceful backwater.

KELD Just off the B6270, Keld is located in a remote and attractive setting at the head of Swaledale nine miles south-east of Kirkby Stephen. Its name is the old Norse word for a spring. The stone houses of Keld are clustered around a chapel and a tiny village square, and the village boasts its own literary institute. The river Swale is fed by many small becks and gills, and just 10 minutes stroll from the village is the beautiful East Gill Force (left). This waterfall is not easily found on many maps and is just north of the Pennine Way where the long-distance footpath crosses East Stonesdale.

Arkengarthdale

The most northern dale in Yorkshire is noted for its scenic attractions. Open skies and panoramic views abound in this remote and beautiful area. The view on the right is from close to the minor road that weaves its way north through the dale alongside Arkle Beck. The road leads to Sleightholme Moor and to the Tan Hill Inn, the highest pub in England which stands at 1732ft (536m) on the border between north Yorkshire and Durham. The pub is often completely cut off in winter weather; partygoers celebrating New Year's Eve at the pub on the last night of 2009 were unable to leave the premises for three days as a result of heavy snowfalls. In 1995 it was the first pub in Britain to be granted a licence to hold weddings.

Langthwaite The largest settlement in Arkengarthdale, Langthwaite's solid stone cottages huddle together haphazardly alongside Arkle Beck, three miles north-west of Reeth in Swaledale. To walk over the packhorse bridge and into the tiny village is like stepping back in time. A popular walk is to stroll through the village and follow the steep single track lane up towards Booze (ironically, a village without a pub!) to soak up the scenery. In the spring there are many wild flowers along this track and as you gain height the views across Arkengarthdale are simply stunning. Looking back over the village the unusual "Waterloo" church of 1817 can be seen. After the French Revolution many churches of this type were built in an attempt to counteract atheism and free thinking. Although the upper fells are scarred with the remains of 18th and 19th-century lead-mining the Dales' place names – Langthwaite, Booze, Arkle, Whaw and Eskeleth – point to their earlier history as Norse settlements. At Slei Gill you can see the remains of a leadmine.

Kisdon Hill The limestone mass of Kisdon Hill stands proud at the western head of Swaledale. The Pennine Way runs round the eastern side of the hill. This viewpoint is from Kisdon Hill looking south towards Muker with the river Swale winding its way along the valley floor. There are many picturesque walks around the area including the long-distance footpath, the Pennine Way. The nearby villages of Keld, Muker and Thwaite offer weary ramblers a welcome break with pretty cottages, tearooms, pubs and interesting lanes to explore at a leisurely pace. The area is famous for its stone walls and field barns. These attractive Dales' barns are situated between Aygill and Thorns Green, just east of the B6270, a minor road that links Thwaite to Keld in Upper Swaledale.

Muker Situated at the head of Swaledale, Muker is about one mile east of Thwaite. It sits proudly above Straw Beck on a long ledge. Muker, Thwaite and Keld are dominated by Kisdon Hill which is over 1,600ft high. Upper Swaledale has some of the finest traditional hay meadows in the whole of the Dales and the setting is breathtaking at any time of year. Muker is the perfect place for walkers to rest on the long-distance footpath, the Pennine Way. The village has a large number of grey stone cottages, a pub, a cafe, and a craft shop. Its buildings of interest include a chapel, an institute and the beautiful church of St Mary the Virgin which was one of only a few built in the reign of Elizabeth I. The colourful east window (below) was given in memory of the Rev Dr HB Wilson, Vicar of Muker (1931-1935). It depicts the scenery around the village, including the river Swale and Straw Beck, together with 23 Swaledale horned sheep – a reference to Psalm 23, *The Lord is my Shepherd*. The Muker Silver Band, formed in 1897 to celebrate Queen Victoria's Diamond Jubilee, is famous throughout the Dales and is one of the last remaining silver bands which once proliferated in this area.

Gunnerside The village of Gunnerside sits at the foot of Gunnerside Gill. It is an unspoilt, picturesque and quiet settlement just three and a half miles east of Thwaite on the B6270, the minor road that links Kirkby Stephen with Richmond. The name "Gunnerside" derives from the Norse for "Gunners Pasture", Gunner being a hero in Norse sagas. It was very conveniently sited for the men who used to work in the many lead mines in the area. The drystone walls, out barns and field system patterns in the valley bottom at Gunnerside are unique and provide photographers and artists with an abundance of opportunities to capture the perfect picture. In June and July the glorious wildflower meadows are a blaze of colour and add greatly to the almost idyllic rural scenery. Gunnerside is at the heart of Swaledale sheep farming and the Dale is famous the world over for its hardy breed of sheep.

Reeth Situated 12 miles west of Richmond, Reeth was once a centre for both leadmining and knitting, and now continues to be the market town for the local community. The village is very popular with tourists and one can easily see why. From its elevated position the spacious village green provides stunning views of the surrounding countryside in Swaledale. The Reeth and District Agricultural Society Show, held annually at the end of August, is a major event in the local calendar.

To the south of Reeth the countryside on either bank of the river Swale is a patchwork of beautiful broad green fields dotted with barns and farm buildings. As you head farther south the land rises abruptly and you are soon on the wild heather fellside of Harkerside Moor. Just above Harkerside Place Farm is the site of an Iron-Age settlement, Maiden Castle Fort. Higher up are the remains of a number of disused leadmines. Further to the east is the preserved Grinton Smelt Mill, which consists of the mill building and a separate peat store. The flue which carried fumes away from the area where the lead was processed can be seen running up the nearby hillside.

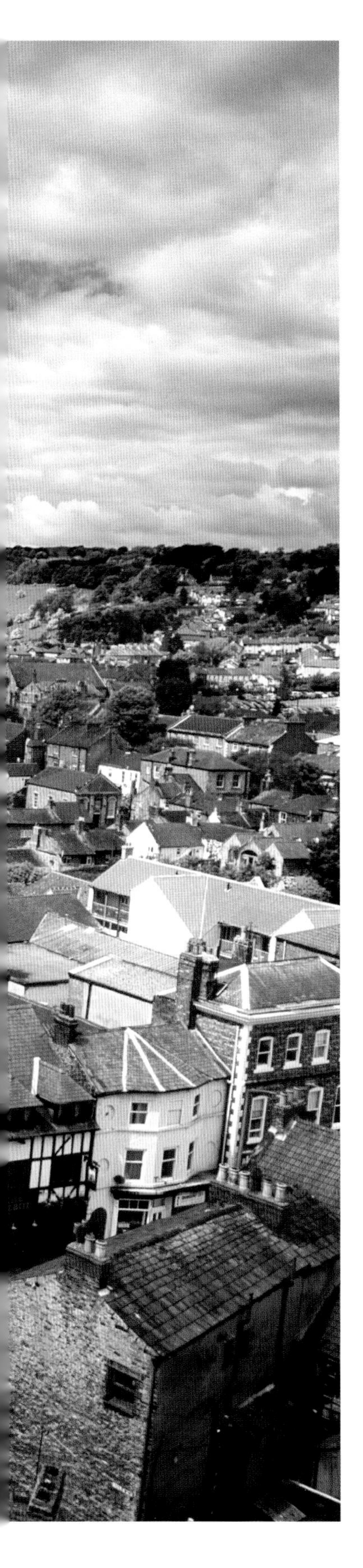

RICHMOND The capital of Swaledale is dominated by its majestic castle keep, a well-preserved piece of 12th-century architecture. The town lies three and a half miles south-west of Scotch Corner on the A6108. Well before the castle was constructed in 1071, Alan Rufus started to build a fortress on the promontory beside the river Swale. The castle we see today, which is 100ft (30m) high and with walls 11ft (3.5m) thick, was built by Alan the Red of Brittany, a trusted supporter of William I, and is one of only a few Norman castles that escaped serious siege damage in later years. The town itself ranks among the most beautiful in England, with many elegant Georgian houses, cobbled streets, and pretty cottage gardens. At the centre of the impressive marketplace is the 12th century chapel of the Holy Trinity, which is now used as the regimental museum of the Green Howards. In 1788, Samuel Butler, a local actor and manager, built a small Georgian theatre called the Theatre Royal. Restored and extended in 2003, it is Britain's most complete Georgian playhouse and is well worth a visit.

Wensleydale

This broad, fertile dale forms an arc cutting through the northern part of the region from east to west.

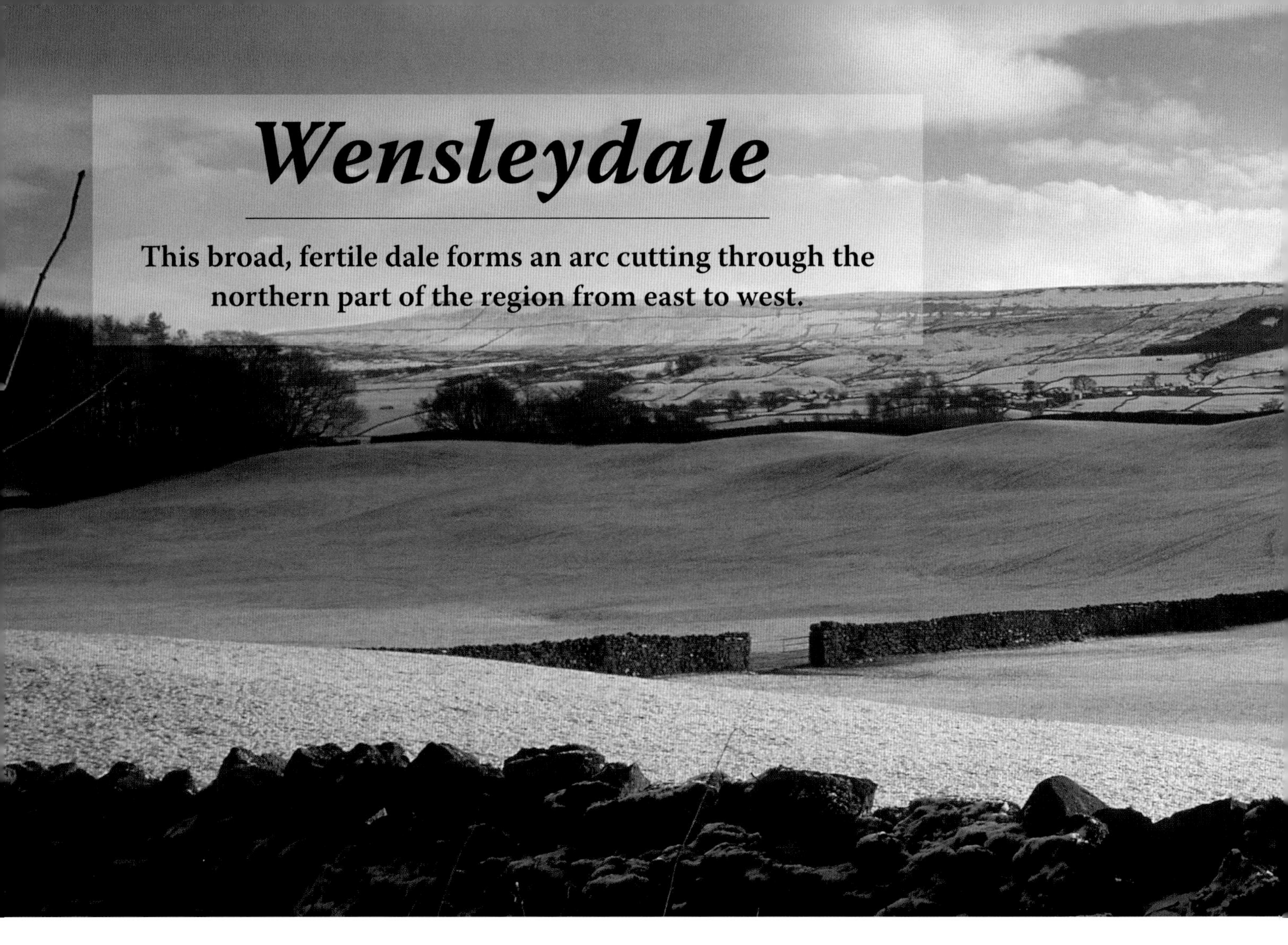

Wensleydale runs from east to west between the busy Wharfedale to the south and the quieter Swaledale to the north. The fellside surrounding the upper river Ure feeds a number of dramatic waterfalls such as those at West Burton and Aysgarth. Further down the dale the countryside is green and open. The market town of Hawes is home to the famous Wensleydale cheese and to the Dales Countryside Museum. To the east a host of beautiful villages such as Castle Bolton, Leyburn and Middleham all have their own marvellous attractions making Wensleydale a popular visitor destination.

Hardraw The village of Hardraw lies one mile north of Hawes on a very quiet by-road, almost at the foot of Buttertubs Pass – a spectacular link road over the fells from Wensleydale to Thwaite in Swaledale. Hardraw is a stopping off point for walkers on the Pennine Way or those embarking on the ascent of nearby Great Shunner Fell, a bleak and remote summit which, at 2,340ft (713m), offers – in good weather – spectacular views of the Three Peaks, Wensleydale and Swaledale. The jewel in the crown at Hardraw is very definitely the 96ft (29m) waterfall, Hardraw Force, said to be the highest in England. Walking to the falls along the banks of Fossdale Gill can be slippery, especially in winter or after rainfall. It is possible to walk behind the shimmering cascade but usually only the most intrepid of visitors will attempt this. Hardraw Force is fed by both Fossdale Gill and Hearne Beck. The falls can only be reached by paying a small access fee and going through the Green Dragon Inn in the centre of the village, but the view is well worth the price! The Green Dragon is also the centre of the Hardraw Gathering – a three-day festival of traditional music, song and dance held at the end of July.

HAWES The busy market town of Hawes sits comfortably between high fells at the head of Wensleydale, on the trans-Pennine A684 that links Northallerton in North Yorkshire to Kendal in Cumbria. Hawes was granted a market charter by William III in 1699. The name Hawes is derived from the word *hause* which means a narrow neck of land. Known as the "little capital" of Upper Wensleydale it is Yorkshire's highest market town and has a thriving farming community. The Hawes Livestock Auction Mart has weekly sales and is always well attended by both locals and visitors. The mart serves a large area of the Yorkshire Dales and the surrounding moorland and fells. The livestock from the area is famed far and wide for its quality. Other enterprising local industries include the unusual Hawes Ropeworks and the Wensleydale Creamery where the famous Wensleydale cheese, first made by local monks in the 12th century, is now produced.

GAYLE Situated just half a mile north of the lively market town of Hawes, Gayle is a quiet and pretty village. At the foot of Sledale, Duerley Beck cascades over a series of limestone steps in the centre of the village before rushing below a packhorse bridge. The broad, sweeping and spectacular landscape of Wensleydale is arguably the most beautiful of all in the Yorkshire Dales. Much of the upper dale can be seen from the packhorse bridge where locals often stop to exchange the news of the day and visitors pause to admire the attractive stepped waterfalls of Duerley Beck. Early spring showers often swell the beck causing a torrent of foaming water to race past the rows of terraced cottages sited on the bank. There is an old cotton mill by the beck, and a stone-flagged causeway leads gently down across meadows to Hawes church. Gayle Mill, situated just downstream from the main bridge, was the winner of the northern heat of the BBC's *Restoration* series in 2004.

Bainbridge The village of Bainbridge, set in the heart of Wensleydale on the A684, has a wide and sweeping village green with ancient village stocks and mature trees, overlooked from the east by the remains of an unexcavated Roman settlement. In Norman times the great forest of Wensleydale dominated the area and forest workers lived in the village. Each evening the Bainbridge hornblower would sound his horn to guide them, and travellers, back to the village. The custom continues to this day: every year from the 27th of September during the Feast of the Holy Rood the horn is still sounded at 10pm. It is kept hanging in the Rose and Crown Inn on the village green. The surrounding area of Upper Wensleydale is well known for its hay meadows, pastures and stone buildings. Artefacts found in earthworks from the Bronze and Iron Age, now kept in the Dales Countryside Museum in Hawes, tell us that Anglian and Norse settlers were farming in these parts centuries ago.

ASKRIGG Just two miles from Bainbridge in Wensleydale, Askrigg sits comfortably below the slopes of Askrigg Common on a quiet minor road that links Leyburn to Hardraw. Askrigg is perhaps best known as the setting for the popular television series *All Creatures Great and Small*. The country vet James Herriot's home Skeldale House in the series is actually Cringly House which can be found in the old market-place. The church of Saint Oswald's, in the centre of the village, is a beautiful 15th-century building with a tall tower, a broad nave and a fine roof. Many of Askrigg's close-packed houses were once used for domestic industries, most notably hand-knitting and clock-making. The skyline across the valley from the village is dominated by the unmistakeable form of Addlebrough – a massive flat-topped hill with imposing crags to its western and northern flanks. The colours and textures on its lower slopes are beautifully high-lighted as the sun sets at the western end of the dale. An annual carnival with parades, music and children's races brings the community together each year in the centre of the village. The young children of the village are seen here setting off to race round the village. Who knows, in years to come, perhaps one will become a fell-race champion!

Aysgarth Located seven miles west of Leyburn on the A684, Aysgarth is probably best known for its spectacular waterfalls that cascade down a series of large limestone steps, making it one of Wensleydale's most popular attractions. A series of delightful riverside walks link the Upper, Middle and Lower Aysgarth Falls. Known collectively as Aysgarth Force, the three sets of falls are all within one mile of each other. The best view of the Upper Falls is from the 16th-century bridge which spans the river Ure. There is a national park information centre and a large car park within easy strolling distance of the falls. In early spring the riverside woodland walks are adorned with a beautiful white carpet of wood anenomes. Aysgarth is in the Deanery of Wensley in the Archdeaconry of Richmond, which is now in the Diocese of Ripon. In earliest times Wensleydale was divided into two main ancient parishes, Aysgarth and Wensley. St Andrew's church, just a few minutes stroll from the falls has, reputedly, the largest churchyard in Britain, which is over four acres in size, together with many outstanding features. Within the church the rood screen (right) was carved by the Ripon School of Carvers in 1506. It is said to have been taken from Jervaulx Abbey after the dissolution of the monasteries in the reign of Henry VIII.

West Burton The pretty, unspoiled village of West Burton is situated one mile south of Aysgarth on the B6160 at the northern end of Bishopdale. The large village green with its unusual village monument and stocks is surrounded by traditional Dales' stone cottages; the small road that runs through the village is unusually peaceful as it comes to a halt alongside Walden Beck. The glorious West Burton Falls, a popular location for artists and photographers, is situated to the east of the village and is easily reached on foot. The upper fall was featured in the film *Robin Hood, Prince of Thieves* starring Kevin Costner in the title role. The scene where Robin tries to ford a river but is stopped by Little John and is forced to fight him is set in and around this picturesque spot. The annual May Fair, on the village green, has something for everyone and is guaranteed to draw the crowds. West Burton schoolchildren can be seen dancing around the maypole, while other attractions include a falconry display, a quoits knockout competition, egg-throwing and morris dancing.

Middleham Just two miles south of Leyburn on the A6108, Middleham is dominated by its ruined castle. The castle was built around 1170 by Robert Fitz Randolph during the reign of Henry II. Although much of the castle was demolished in the 17th century, the keep is still an imposing structure which can be seen for miles around; it has 12ft (3.5m) thick walls and is one of the largest in England. There has been a settlement at Middleham since Roman times and in the Domesday Book it is known as *Medelai*. In 1985 Ted Seaton was using a metal-detector near the castle when he discovered a gold pendant weighing 2.3 ounces (68g) together with a magnificent blue sapphire. The pendant dated from the 15th-century and is now known as the Middleham Jewel; when it was sold at auction it reached the amazing sum of £1.3m. The Yorkshire Museum, in York, has since raised £2.5m to acquire the now world-famous jewel. In a low-lying position between Coverdale and Wensleydale the town has long been a centre for the training of racehorses. The Middleham Trainers Association represents trainers in the town and district, in the whole of North Yorkshire and England.

West Witton Just four miles west of Leyburn on the A684, West Witton sits comfortably in the lee of Penhill which dominates the skyline in this part of Wensleydale. Wensleydale is the largest of all the Dales, a broad sweeping fertile valley in its lower reaches, which gradually closes in as you travel up the dale. At the head of Wensleydale, in the area around Hawes, the landscape is more dramatic with steeper slopes leading to high windswept fells and remote winding mountain pass roads. The photograph (below) over the gate was taken from the minor road that climbs steeply out of the village to the south and up past Penhill Farm to Melmerby. The field just beyond the gate, which belongs to Penhill Farm, is called "Bella Field". In centuries past, the whole of this part of Wensleydale was forested. The parish church of St Bartholomew was originally Saxon, and possibly built in the sixth century. When the church was restored in 1875 the remains of a Saxon cross were found in the chancel walls. Interestingly, before 1752, the dead from West Witton were taken to Wensley for burial because the shallow depth of soil in the churchyard meant that graves could not be dug successfully. Later, extra soil was brought in to alleviate the problem.

Leyburn The attractive town of Leyburn developed quite naturally as a market town since it is situated on the important A684 trans-Pennine route between Kendal in Cumbria and Northallerton in North Yorkshire at the junction of four main roads. Although Leyburn is the main commercial, market and trading centre for lower Wensleydale, it did not receive its charter until 1684. The area is well-known for fabulous views of Wensleydale from Leyburn Shawl, a grassy terrace high above the valley to the west of the town which is easily reached from Shawl Terrace at the top of the Market Place. The people of Leyburn certainly know how to celebrate. Each year at the beginning of May the town hosts the Dales Festival of Food and Drink. This event has developed into a popular festival lasting three days. The Richmond Pipe Band can always be relied upon to thrill and entertain at this and many other events in the area. The Elite Cinema (above) is a small independent venue showing a varied programme from art-house to Hollywood. There is a comfortable bar, and occasionally live theatre and music is staged. The auditorium seats 173 people. Leyburn is two miles from its near neighbour Middleham, and the two villages are linked by a suspension bridge. One of the first suspension bridges to be constructed, it was built in 1829 to ford the river Ure. Leyburn railway station offers trips on the recently refurbished Wensleydale Line which runs from Leeming Bar to Redmire, a distance of 16 miles.

Redmire Five miles west of Leyburn lies Redmire, on the minor road that runs along the northern side of Wensleydale. In centuries past the village was a hive of industry and both coal and lead were mined locally; the legacy of this activity is clearly visible in the landscape to the north of the village above nearby Castle Bolton. Today's visitors will find that all traces of Redmire's industrial past have now given way to delightful cottage gardens, resplendent with flowers and vegetables. This charming, peaceful village, with its hidden nooks, crannies and riverside haunts deserves to be explored on foot. Several narrow lanes lead off the small village green which is dominated by a huge and ancient oak tree; the one which passes the smithy and the Bolton Arms leads to Castle Bolton and the road up and over the moor to Grinton in Swaledale.

Castle Bolton The small village of Castle Bolton, five miles west of Leyburn, is dominated by Bolton Castle. There is a wide green in the centre of the village and an attractive 14th-century church, St Oswald's, nestles in the shadow of this impressive structure. The massive fortress of Bolton Castle has dominated Wensleydale since 1379 and can be seen for miles around. It is one of the country's best preserved castles; Mary Queen of Scots was imprisoned here during 1568 and 1569. The photograph (left) looking south across Wensleydale was taken from its delightful herb garden. Two of the castle gardens, the Herb Garden and the Walled Garden, have been restored along medieval lines, and should not be missed, providing visitors with a beautiful setting and wonderful views of the dale. The village of Grinton in Swaledale, with its interesting church and picturesque Bridge Inn, can be reached from a minor moor road at the eastern end of the village.

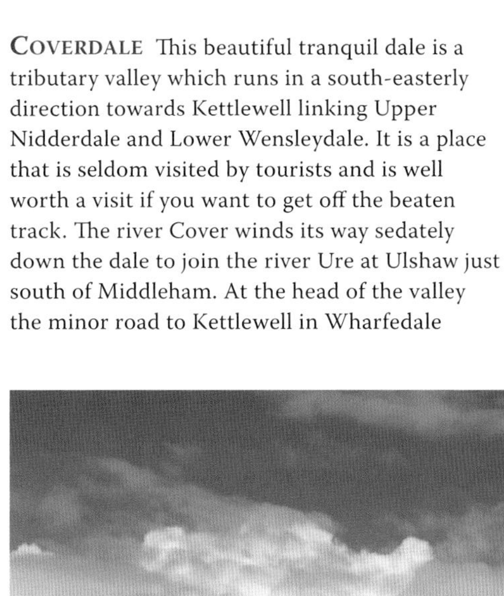

COVERDALE This beautiful tranquil dale is a tributary valley which runs in a south-easterly direction towards Kettlewell linking Upper Nidderdale and Lower Wensleydale. It is a place that is seldom visited by tourists and is well worth a visit if you want to get off the beaten track. The river Cover winds its way sedately down the dale to join the river Ure at Ulshaw just south of Middleham. At the head of the valley the minor road to Kettlewell in Wharfedale passes through Coverhead between Great Whernside (2310ft/704m) and Buckden Pike (2303ft/702m); this is a wild and windswept spot but one that offers dramatic panoramic views back down Coverdale towards Middleham. Halfway down the dale the pretty hamlets of Carlton and Horsehouse sit admidst superb farming and walking country just a short drive from the nearby Dales' towns of Richmond, Leyburn, Hawes and Middleham.

Dentdale & Ribblesdale

These two western Dales straddle the border with Cumbria giving this region its own distinct personality, ranging from lush green valleys to wild, windswept moorland.

With its white-painted houses and softly rounded fells, Dentdale shares many characteristics with the Lake District which it borders. Ribblesdale, to the south, is at the heart of Three Peaks Country (named after the three mountains of Pen-y-Ghent, Whernside and Ingleborough) and has some of the most outstanding limestone scenery in Britain. Linking the area is the Settle to Carlisle railway line, one of the most dramatic and scenic rail routes in Europe.

Howgill Fells Taken from the roadside near the Cross Keys Inn on the Sedbergh to Kirkby Stephen road, this is one of the best views of the Howgills, a small distinctive group of hills bordered by Sedbergh, Kirkby Stephen and Tebay. The southern half of the Howgills lie in the Yorkshire Dales National Park, whilst the northern Howgills are in Cumbria. In their centre lies Cautley Spout, Britain's highest waterfall, where Red Gill Beck tumbles over the edge of Cautley Crags from the shoulder of the Calf – the highest of the Howgill Fells at 2217ft (676m). The buildings shown on the left are at Low Haygarth Farm which is in regular use as a trekking and trail-riding centre with the distinctive rounded Howgill Fells forming a backdrop.

Dent Four miles south-east of Sedbergh the pretty village of Dent is actually in Cumbria, although it lies within the Yorkshire Dales National Park. It boasts the highest mainline railway station in Britain (four miles from the village) and is close to the spectacular viaducts of Arten Gill and Dent Head on the Settle-Carlisle railway line. Strolling through the narrow cobbled streets of Dent is like travelling back in time. The white-painted cottages (below) are most unusual and very Cumbrian in character. Dent was immortalised in the poem by Robert Southey entitled *The Terrible Knitters o' Dent* – so-called because of the villagers' prodigious output of knitwear. At one time everyone in the village knitted in order to supplement their meagre incomes, and the stockings and nightcaps produced were

sold locally or taken further afield. A visit to the Dentdale Heritage Centre gives an opportunity to discover more about the working lives of the villagers in centuries past. In the centre of the village can be found a huge slab of Shap granite (above). This is a memorial to Adam Sedgwick, a native of Dent who went on to become a professor of geology at Cambridge. Cool spring water flows out into a small trough at the base of the monument and provides a welcome drink after walking on the fells or exploring the cobbled streets.

Dentdale Farms and cottages in Dentdale are almost always painted white, in the Cumbrian style, in contrast to the warm natural stone buildings usually found in the lower Yorkshire Dales. The photograph above looks north-west from just below Combe Scar on a clear day. In the distance the Howgill Fells can be seen clearly on the horizon and in the middle distance are Helms Knott and Long Rigg ridge.

Brigflatts The Quaker Friends Meeting House (below) is at Brigflatts, half a mile from Sedbergh on the A683 Kirkby Lonsdale road. The meeting house was built in 1675 at a time when the village was a thriving and mostly self-sufficient community of around 75 people who ran their own cottage industry relying principally on flax weaving.

Ingleton The pretty market town of Ingleton is set amidst the unique landscape of the limestone uplands of the Dales. Situated just six miles south-east of Kirkby Lonsdale, it is by-passed by the A65 which follows the route of the historic Keighley-Kendal turnpike. Ingleton nestles in the lee of Ingleborough, one of the famous Three Peaks of the Yorkshire Dales, the others being Pen-y-Ghent and Whernside. The settlement is surrounded by dramatic scenery both below and above ground. The Ingleton waterfalls provide visitors with an amazing series of cascades tumbling down through wooded gorges. White Scar Cave, a short distance north-east of the village on the lower slopes of Ingleborough, is the longest show cave in Britain. The cave boasts an amazing subterranean landscape with thousands of stalactites and rushing streams, exotic cave formations and a massive Ice-Age cavern. In the village narrow winding streets are clustered around a tiny marketplace. Nearby, the late Victorian church of St Mary's has one of the finest Norman fonts in Yorkshire. There are many hotels, guesthouses and a youth hostel, and golfers will find that there are fantastic views of the area from Ingleton golf course. St Mary's can be seen here overlooking Bell Horse Gate cottages. Wool and cotton-spinning were very important local industries in the 18th and 19th centuries, and many more terraced workers' cottages are to be found in the shadow of the magnificent Ingleton Viaduct at the bottom of this steep hill. The photograph (top right) was taken from the Millennium 2000 garden which is landscaped into the hillside.

Ingleton Waterfalls Walk Just north of the town is some of the best waterfall and woodland scenery in the north of England. Here two rivers meet – the Twiss flows down Kingsdale and the Doe from Chapel-le-Dale. Both rivers cascade through a series of waterfalls and plunge pools. A circular trail of around 4.5miles (8km) – the Waterfalls Walk – takes you along the banks of both rivers, first the river Twiss and then returning down the river Doe. The largest and most famous waterfall, Thornton Force, plunges 14 metres (46ft) over a cliff of limestone on the river Twiss just north of the equally spectacular Pecca Falls. On the river Doe there are also a number of attractive waterfalls such as the Beezley and Snow Falls as well as the Rival Falls which offers views of the river plunging into a deep pool known locally as the black hole. The final part of the walk takes you past old limestone workings and limekilns before emerging into Ingleton village. There is an entrance fee to walk the trail which was first opened to the public in 1885.

Ingleborough The unique and spectacular limestone uplands of the Dales contain three neighbouring peaks, Ingleborough, Pen-y-Ghent and Whernside, known as the Three Peaks. Ingleborough, the second highest, is pictured top right from just below Runscar Hill, shrouded in low cloud on a bitterly cold winter's day. The lower slopes have many caves and potholes and include the cavernous Gaping Gill Pot on the western flank of the mountain.

Kingsdale In the heart of Three Peaks limestone country are these two massive boulders, known as the Cheese Press Stones. They are a reminder of the time when cheese was pressed into shape between large stones when it was drying out.

SETTLE Situated just off the busy A65 Keighley to Kendal road, on the B6480 that runs northwards through Ribblesdale, the market town of Settle is a focal point for the district and popular with visitors. Settle's market charter goes back to 1249, and together with nearby Clapham and Ribblesdale it has a close association with the famous Settle to Carlisle Railway line. The town has developed and prospered due to its location, being surrounded by mixed and arable farming together with some quite spectacular limestone scenery. It sits snugly between the river Ribble and towering limestone crags. Immediately overlooking the town is Castlebergh, an impressive 300ft (91m) limestone crag, and to the east is Malham with its unique scenery of tarns and limestone pavements. The market square is surrounded by 18th and 19th-century houses, shops, arcades and courtyards. The Naked Man Café, so popular with touring motorcyclists and visitors, is an enigma, as no one seems to know why the carved, almost naked, man is there. Scalebar Force, a beautiful cascading waterfall, is located just a couple of miles from the town centre and a short walk from the minor road that leads to Kirkby Malham. Unusually Settle did not have an ancient church, and so locals had to go to the church of St Akelda in nearby Giggleswick to worship. Today the parish is served by the church of the Holy Ascension in Settle, the church of St Akelda in Giggleswick and Holy Trinity in Rathmell.

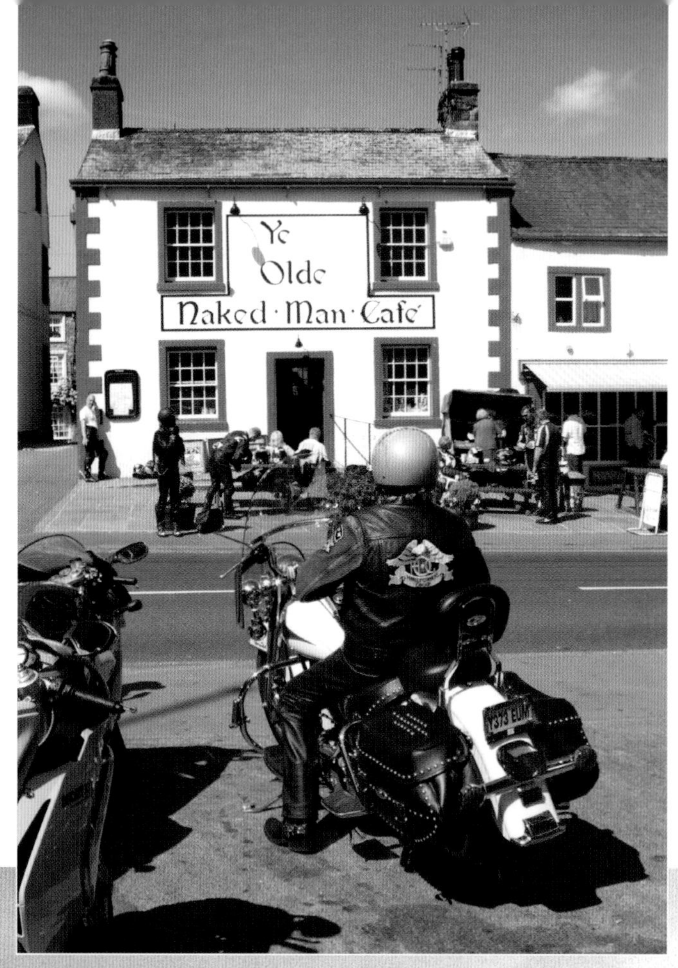

Ribblehead Viaduct
The 72-mile Settle to Carlisle railway line is one of the most picturesque in Britain and runs the length of Ribblesdale, with dramatic views of both Whernside and Pen-y-Ghent. This magnificent viaduct is just to the west of Ribblehead station. Built between 1870 and 1875 it is 104ft high, 1200ft long and has 24 arches. The Settle-Carlisle line was the last great mainline railway route to be built in England and consists of 72 miles of track with 17 major viaducts spanning the ravines and 14 tunnels.

Stainforth The small and peaceful village of Stainforth, now by-passed by the B6479, lies just two miles north of Settle. The name Stainforth is derived from the "stony ford" which once linked two separate settlements on opposite sides of the river Ribble. The narrow, high-arched 17th-century packhorse bridge (far left) replaced the ford from which the village got its name and is now owned by the National Trust. The broad stone ledges provide a very popular picnic site for visitors, and early spring showers swell the rapids as they gush over Stainforth Force. Banks of bluebells and fresh green foliage combine to make a delightful riverside setting. Stainforth Beck flows down from Catrigg Force just one mile from the village. The waterfall is easily reached along a stony track to the east and ancient stepping stones across the beck provide relatively easy access from the centre of the village. St Peter's church is situated in Great Stainforth, or Stainforth-under-Bargh as it used to be known (literally "the stony ford under the hill") on the east bank of the river. Prior to the middle of the 19th century Stainforth had no church of its own, belonging to the neighbouring parish of Giggleswick.

Ribblesdale This bleak winter scene near Horton in Ribblesdale shows how the beautiful scenery of the upper dales can change suddenly when winter weather sweeps in. The photograph below is taken from the Pennine Way long-distance footpath on the remote Stainforth to Littondale road. This dramatic view of Pen-y-Ghent almost entices the viewer to tackle this famous peak. The route of the Pennine Way follows this dead-end track for a short distance, then goes up and over the summit of Pen-y-Ghent, down to the village of Horton in Ribblesdale and then north to Hawes in Wensleydale. The lowest of the Three Peaks, Pen-y-Ghent's towering cliffs and escarpments more than make up for its lack of height. The three broad, bare faces on the western side of the mountain were shaped during a dramatic thunderstorm in July 1881 when the surface soil was washed away.

Clapham This is a blissful haven for visitors just off the busy A65 six miles north-west of Settle. It is a focal point for walks to Selside, Austwick and Horton-in-Ribblesdale. It is also a perfect base for exploring the remote and beautiful Crummackdale where the famous Norber erratic boulders are located. The beautiful Clapham Beck flows through the centre of the village, and passes beneath four bridges. The village is much more wooded than most other Dales' villages, thanks mainly to the Farrer family who, in the early 18th century, developed Clapham as an estate village. Ingleborough Hall was rebuilt, and Clapham Beck was planted with thousands of trees. The beck was dammed to create a lake which changed the character of the top part of the village. Close by stands the Church of St James which was founded in Norman times. The angel window display in the porch, together with many more displays in the church, were part of the Myths and Legends Festival in the year 2004. The festival celebrated the 50th anniversary of the Yorkshire Dales becoming a national park.

Horton in Ribblesdale The start and finishing point of the famous Three Peaks Walk, Horton is also a popular stopping place for walkers tackling the Pennine Way. The local cafe provides much more than large pots of Yorkshire tea; it is also the place where Three Peaks' walkers clock in and out to register their progress on the walk. Each year there is a large entry of competitors in the famous Three Peaks fell race which takes place during the Horton Gala. The fastest runners will cover the 24-mile distance in just under three hours.

CRUMMACK
CLAPHAM

Crummackdale This tiny dale, barely five miles long, is tucked away between Ribblesdale and Ingleborough. It contains some of the finest fell and limestone scenery in the Dales. Norber Fell, literally North Hill (above) is a sloping plateau of land just north of the village of Austwick. The fell is best known for the Norber "erratics" – sandstone boulders of varying sizes which were deposited by glacial action on the limestone fellside. A number of these can be seen in the photograph on the left. The erratics immediately look out of place on the hillside which is a mixture of grassland and limestone pavement. This is accentuated by the fact that the sandstone erratics are usually covered in green lichen whilst the limestone attracts white lichen. When the erratics sit directly on top of the limestone pavement, erosion of both the sandstone and the limestone often results in huge sandstone blocks perched on top of tiny supporting limestone boulders. Just to the east of Norber Fell lies the hamlet of Horton in Ribblesdale. Horton's pretty station, on the Settle-Carlisle line, won the Best Kept Station award for 17 consecutive years in the 1950s and 60s. With its neat, well-maintained gardens and brightly painted woodwork, it has all the hallmarks of a classic railway station from the golden age of steam.

Malhamdale & Littondale

Busy Malhamdale is famous for its limestone scenery, while Littondale to the north remains a quiet, peaceful backwater.

The unique limestone landscape of Malhamdale, which was formed over millions of years, first by glacial erosion and then by the effects of wind, rain and frost, makes for a great visitor destination. Two of the best features – the limestone cliff at Malham Cove and Malham Tarn – are sited behind the attractive village of Malham. Above the Cove lies Malham pavement (right) where hundreds of limestone blocks or "clints" are criss-crossed with deep fissures or "grykes". Just a few miles north-east of Malham is the dramatic limestone ravine of Goredale Scar, which has inspired poets and painters for hundreds of years.

Malham and Malhamdale Surrounded by some of the most beautiful and spectacular landscape features in the British Isles, Malhamdale is always popular. The village lies just five miles west of Settle and two and a half miles south of Malham Tarn on the Pennine Way. Malham Cove, Gordale Scar, Janet's Foss Waterfall (right) and Malham Tarn are all located at 1,229ft (375m) above sea level. They are all unique and impressive landscape features. Malham Cove is just three-quarters of a mile north of the village, and at 250ft (76m) high and over 300 yards (275m) long, is a magnificent vertical limestone rockface. At the base of the cove, as if by magic, Malham Beck appears then flows gently down through the village before making its way into the river Aire. Malham Tarn is a very large lake formed by glaciation in the last ice age, with abundant birdlife, making it attractive to birdwatchers. It is the highest lake in England. Charles Kingsley, a regular visitor to the area, set the opening scenes of his classic children's novel *The Water Babies* here and wrote much of the novel close to Malham. Visitors flock to the nature reserve at the tarn and the walks around the tarn are delightful. There is a National Trust visitor centre at Tarn House.

Arncliffe The village of Arncliffe lies at the heart of Littondale, one of the loveliest of the Dales. It is the largest of the four settlements in the dale, which include the village of Litton and the small hamlets of Halton Gill and remote Foxup. Just six miles north-west of Grassington, Arncliffe sits comfortably by the river Skirfare on a well-drained gravel delta above the flood plain. Arncliffe has a central wide open green, surrounded by mellow stone cottages and farm buildings. Several large porched barns point to the fact that this is a typical Dales' working community. The days of muckspreading by hand from horse and cart, and taking hay to the fields on horseback, are distant memories now and a far more familiar sound is that of the quad bike. Littondale was the setting for part of Charles Kingsley's novel *The Water Babies*, and it was also chosen originally as the setting for the long-running and popular television series *Emmerdale*. A much-loved characteristic of the village is the large number of hardwood trees that surround the church and stretch along both sides of the river bank.

GORDALE SCAR One mile north-east of Malham, the limestone escarpment opens up into a huge rocky gorge known as Gordale Scar. This massive ravine was gouged out of the landscape by melting glaciers during the Ice Age (15-16 million years ago) and the 100m high overhanging cliffs make it one of the most spectacular sights in the Dales. Gordale Beck cascades over two waterfalls as it makes its way through the gorge. The beck then leaves the gorge and shortly afterwards tumbles over a limestone outcrop into a deep pool known as Janet's Foss, which in the past was used for sheep dipping. Gordale Spa has been a great source of inspiration for writers and artists, particularly the Romantics. The poet Thomas Gray said that it was almost impossible to stay in Gordale Scar for more than a quarter of an hour without shuddering. William Wordsworth visited the area in 1819 and wrote a sonnet to Gordale describing the shadowy light effects in the gorge, particularly at dawn or sunset. James Ward, one of the greatest British painters of the early 19th century, painted Gordale Spa in 1814-15; this giant painting now hangs in Tate Britain, London and is regarded as Ward's masterpiece and one of the key paintings of the Romantic period.

FOXUP There are four small settlements in Littondale – Arncliffe, Litton, Halton Gill and Foxup, which is the most remote. The hamlet is made up of a scattering of small cottages and farms, close to where Foxup Beck feeds the infant river Skirfare.

Halton Gill Situated at the northern end of Littondale and eight miles north-east of Settle, Halton Gill has a beautiful and quite spectacular setting. Surrounded and sheltered by Plover Hill, Cow Close Fell and Horse Head Moor, the village of Halton Gill sits beside the infant river Skirfare, which is fed by Cosh Beck, Foxup Beck and Hesleden Beck. The stone houses and farm buildings are mostly 17th century and one barn has a huge entrance porch dated 1829. The 17th-century chapel in the village is combined with the schoolhouse. The village can be seen over the gate from the footpath to Foxup. Just above the two villages, at the confluence of the two streams which combine to make the Skirfare, is the lonely farmstead of Cosh House, said to be the most isolated dwelling in the Dales. This area has a strong link with those who fought the Scots at Flodden Field.

Langstrothdale, Wharfedale & Nidderdale

These dales, located to the south of the region, run parallel to each other in a north-west to south-easterly direction.

From Buckden down to Bolton Abbey the magnificent upland scenery of Wharfedale includes the massive bulk of Great Whernside, Buckden Pike and the stunning limestone slopes of Kilnsey Crag. Nidderdale, one of the shortest of the main dales, has a great deal of interest including the settlements of Middlesmoor and Pateley Bridge, and the Gouthwaite Reservoir. The upper valley of the Wharfe above Buckden is known as Langstrothdale. The tiny hamlet of Yockenthwaite (above) is typical of the small settlements found in Langstrothdale. The scene on the left shows Wharfedale from Hill Castles Scar. This photograph was taken near the Dales Way footpath, between Kettlewell and Grassington, just north-east of the village of Conistone in Wharfedale. The view towards Hawkswick Moor and Middlesmoor Pasture is breathtaking, especially when weather systems are racing across the dales, creating atmospheric and dramatic skies.

YOCKENTHWAITE The tiny, picturesque hamlet of Yockenthwaite, nestling on the hillside beside the infant river Wharfe, is now merely a scattering of stone barns and traditional Dales' houses. It is, though, an ancient settlement with a Norse-Celtic name which means Egon's Clearing. A short distance upstream can be found one of only a few Bronze Age stone circles in the Dales. It has 20 stones and is approximately 25ft (7.6m) in diameter. In Norman times Langstrothdale Chase (the upper valley of the Wharfe) was a hunting preserve for game and deer, with its own forest laws, courts, punishments and privileges.

HUBBERHOLME This tiny village is located on the Dales Way four and a half miles from Kettlewell and is famous for its beautiful church and pub. Named after a Viking chieftain, and situated at the foot of Langstrothdale, the village consists of a cluster of old farm cottages surrounding the church – St Michael and All Angels – and the George Inn, pictured here beyond the bridge. Hubberholme was the favourite village of the great Yorkshire writer JB Priestley. Literary pilgrims make a beeline for the pub, where he could often be found enjoying the local ale, and the churchyard, the last resting place for his ashes. The loft in the church roof dates from 1558 and is one of very few of this type left in England. The choir stalls and the pews are more recent and were made in 1934 by Robert Thompson, the "Mouseman" of Kilburn. The George Inn was once a vicarage, and its outside lavatories have quaint signs to guide users so that Y'ewes and Tups do not get confused. Spring Bank Holiday weekend heralds the welcome return of Morris dancers (below) who fill the air with lively music and laughter.

BUCKDEN The village of Buckden, four miles north of Kettlewell on the B6160, is very popular with walkers; paths lead from the village in all directions, making it the perfect base for exploring Wharfedale with its glorious scenery. The annual Buckden Pike Fell Race is a great draw for runners from across the north of England, and it is an exciting spectacle to see such fit athletes powering their way up steep inclines. The race is four miles (6.4km) long and finishes on the gala field after a climb of 1,500ft (450m) to the top and back. To amble through Wharfedale's glorious wildflower meadows in spring is a memorable experience. Starting from the village, a much-loved triangular walk of approximately seven miles takes in the small hamlets of Cray, Yockenthwaite and Hubberholme. Part of the walk includes a short section of Roman road along

Great Whernside This rugged hill (left) dominates the skyline to the east of Buckden. Not to be confused with Whernside (one of the Three Peaks further to the west) it reaches a height of 2310ft and creates an abrupt change from the lush pastures in the valley below. The long boulder-strewn ridge gives extensive views across Nidderdale to the east and westward to Wharfedale.

Buckden Rake which provides superb views west across the head of Wharfedale into Langstrothdale from a gallery footpath on a natural limestone shelf. Close to the summit of Buckden Pike is a memorial to the Polish crew of an aircraft that crashed here in 1942. The sole survivor managed to reach safety by following the tracks of a fox in the snow.

CRAY The little hamlet of Cray nestles at the southern end of Bishopdale one and a half miles north of Buckden. It is the starting point for many walks and its famous inn, The White Lion, is the highest pub in Wharfedale. Cray consists of a scatter of stone houses and farm buildings and is situated about halfway up Buckden Pike, below Kidstones Pass. It is very accessible from Skipton, lying as it does on the B6160 between Wharfedale and Wensleydale. It is a useful starting point for ramblers and could provide an overnight stop for those walking the Dales Way. The barn in the photograph is typical of those in the southern dales, many of which were built between 1750 and 1850. Barn walls are very similar in construction to the drystone walls of the fields – two faced edges are placed together with a packing of smaller stones and bonding stones. Cray Gill runs into the river Wharfe a couple of miles south of the village and is fed by several smaller gills which cascade over rocky outcrops forming beautiful waterfalls.

Kettlewell In the shadow of Great Whernside 13 miles north of Skipton, Kettlewell is popular with potholers, climbers and walkers. Its buildings are clustered close to Cam Beck, near where it joins the river Wharfe. The Scarecrow Festival in Kettlewell (below) has become an increasingly popular community event, attracting ever more visitors to this delightful village each year. Kettlewell's beautiful setting is an ideal place from which to explore the surrounding fells and the river valley. Many of the stone houses in the village which stand on the banks of the Wharfe or Kettlewell Beck date from the 17th and 18th centuries. Although the village green no longer exists, the spot is marked by a distinctive white maypole close to the centre of the village. Kettlewell is popular with visitors and there are numerous holiday cottages, pubs and restaurants including The Racehorses Hotel, the Bluebell Inn and the King's Head. The beautiful fields (above) lie just south of the village and were photographed from a footpath just above Crookacre Wood. Low winter sunshine reveals the distinctive pattern of drystone walls and out barns, so typical of the area. The long-distance footpath, the Dales Way, which links Ilkley to Windermere, runs along the valley bottom at this point.

Kilnsey The tiny village of Kilnsey lies just three miles north of Grassington on the B6160 in the heart of Wharfedale. It nestles in the shadow of Kilnsey Crag, a dramatic limestone peak much loved by climbers. Together with its glorious setting, Kilnsey has many attractions. These include the long-distance footpath, the Dales Way, which passes close by, and pony-trekking from the village of Conistone just half a mile away across the valley. There is also fly-fishing and a nature trail at Kilnsey Park Trout Farm. The popular Tennant Arms provides a warm and friendly welcome, so typical of Dales' pubs. Kilnsey Crag towers high over the village – 170ft (52m) above the nearby B6160 – and is the most prominent landmark in Wharfedale. The 40ft (12m) overhang at the top provides an irresistible challenge to climbers and passing walkers are often to be seen gazing up in astonishment at their daring and agility. The Kilnsey Agricultural Show is a showcase for the local farming community. Organised by the Upper Wharfedale Agricultural Society it has a proud history stretching back over 100 years. It takes place on the Tuesday after the August Bank Holiday against the backdrop of Kilnsey Crag, and is the ideal opportunity for the older characters of the dale to get together and catch up on local news and events.

Linton Seven miles north of Skipton, the characterful village of Linton consists of stone cottages built in clusters around the village green. The green slopes eastwards towards the grassy banks of Linton Beck. There are many elegant houses in this picturesque village; a particularly unusual building by the green, the Fontaine Hospital, was built in 1721 as almshouses for six poor men or women. Linton was voted the "prettiest village in the North" in 1949 and it appears that very little has changed since then. Linton Beck flows through the middle of the village and is crossed by a packhorse bridge, a modern road bridge, a clapper bridge, stepping stones and fords. Visitors who venture just a mile from the village will discover waterfalls, a weir, riverside paths and the delightful St Michael's church beside the river Wharfe. There is always a warm welcome at the Fontaine Inn, which overlooks the village green.

GRASSINGTON The largest settlement in upper Wharfedale, Grassington has developed mainly due to its close proximity to the point where two historically important roads cross in the dale. The B6160 from Ilkley to Buckden and beyond meets the B6265 Skipton to Pateley Bridge at Threshfield, just east of the village. Grassington has many charming features including a cobbled square complete with an ornate water pump, restored in the year 2000 to commemorate the men in the village who lost their lives in the First and Second World Wars. The village was granted a charter for a market and fair in 1281, and this continued to be held until about 1860. Today's farmers' market is a thriving concern and at Christmas the shopkeepers in the village dress in Dickensian costume and transform Grassington into a Victorian village. Grass Wood, a large area of ancient woodland which includes the Iron-Age fort, Fort Gregory, is situated just over one mile north-west of Grassington.

BURNSALL Ten miles north-west of Ilkley, Burnsall is famous for its massive five-arched bridge which spans the river Wharfe. The bridge was built by Sir William Craven, who also restored the local parish church and endowed the local grammar school. The bridge is probably the most photographed in the Dales. Every August the village of Burnsall hosts England's oldest fell race. This event is tremendously popular, with both locals and visitors alike. There is a wonderful carnival atmosphere to be experienced throughout the day, usually with a brass band playing. Family races and many other traditional community country sports take place on the village green. Burnsall is everything a Dales' village should be, and its shape is very much dictated by the river Wharfe. Many of the houses date back to the 17th century and are built from rich warm stone. The photograph of the village in the winter (below) was taken from Rowan Tree Crag shortly after sunrise in February. A trip to the Dales would not be complete without visiting one of the many outstanding churches, and Wharfedale has its fair share of them. The parish church of St Wilfred is a fine example and can be approached via a unique lych-gate. The church was founded in the 12th century by de Romilles of Skipton. This 19th-century stained-glass panel (right) is a memorial to William Stockdale (1747-1836) and his wife Sarah (1768-1848).

HEBDEN The small village of Hebden lies on the road to Pateley Bridge and Nidderdale about two miles east of Grassington. Located in an upland valley it is surrounded by rocky crags and picturesque waterfalls. It sits proudly above its beck within a narrow gorge, which is unusual for this area in exposing dark gritstone rock rather than the more familiar limestone. Hebden Brook runs through the village as it makes its way down to the river Wharfe. A quaint packhorse bridge (below) leads over the brook to an idyllic cluster of stone cottages. Beyond these cottages several paths lead up onto Hebden Moor where there are many disused mines and shafts. The Village Store and Post Office (left) provide a much needed service to the local community, and in high summer a very welcome Yorkshire Dales Old Fashioned Dairy Ice Cream!

Appletreewick Four miles south-east of Grassington, this peaceful Wharfedale village rests on a steep slope overlooked by the craggy summit of Simon's Seat. The main street is lined with ornate and characterful cottages and at either end there is Low Hall and High Hall. Sir William Craven, Appletreewick's most famous inhabitant, was known as "Dick Whittington of the Dales". A farmer's son, he was sent to London to make his fortune. He became Lord Mayor in 1610! Sir William rebuilt High Hall and the building is still to be found at the top of the hill. The local community in Appletreewick pride themselves on the fact that almost all of the properties are occupied by residents living in the village. They enjoy the benefit of having two public houses, cricket, darts and domino teams as well as the small but beautiful church of St John's. As can be seen (left), Appletreewick nestles snugly on a south-facing slope above the river Wharfe and is surrounded by some of the most beautiful scenery in Wharfedale; to the right is the summit of Simon's Seat. This photograph was taken from the slopes of Burnsall Fell. The very distinctive Mock Beggar Hall (below) in the centre of the village was built on the site of a grange used by the monks of Bolton Priory. It is rumoured that one particularly wayward monk was walled up inside the hall.

Simon's Seat and Skyreholme The rocky summit of Simon's Seat dominates the skyline to the south-east of Appletreewick. From the triangulation point which marks Simon's Seat there are excellent views to the valley below around Appletreewick; amongst the trees is the ancient Parcevall Hall at the foot of Troller's Gill. The narrow limestone gorge of Troller's Gill is said to be the haunt of the "Barquest", a terrifying hound with huge staring eyes which may have been the inspiration for the Sherlock Holmes story *The Hound of the Baskervilles.* From the summit you can also look north into Skyredale and the tiny hamlets of Skyreholme and Upper Skyreholme. Parcevall Hall lies on a steep hillside and has the only RHS and English Heritage registered gardens open to the public in the Yorkshire Dales National Park. The gardens were laid out by Sir William Milner from 1927 onwards, and are planted with many specimen trees and shrubs collected from Western China and the Himalayas. The cruck barn (below) is part of the Craven Arms, a 16th century inn north-west of Appletreewick.

Bolton Abbey Bolton Bridge, on the A59 just five miles west of Skipton, is the gateway to Wharfedale. It is just a stone's throw from Bolton Abbey, a beautiful Augustinian priory. The abbey was founded in 1151 on land given by Lady Alice de Romille of Skipton Castle. In the early 14th century the abbey was reduced to ruins by Scottish raiders although the nave of the church was still used as a parish church until the Dissolution of the Monasteries, from 1536 onwards. Bolton Abbey is very popular with visitors, many of whom linger close to the monastic buildings, often choosing to picnic and spend a day by the river. Those who venture a little further along the splendid riverside walks will find some of Wharfedale's most popular attractions. Two of the most spectacular are "the Strid" – the narrow chasm through which the river Wharfe gushes in a thunderous cascade – and the enchanting Valley of Desolation with its waterfalls and wooded glades. Further upstream, along a nature trail, can be found Barden Bridge and the beautifully sited Barden Tower, a ruined hunting lodge, which was built in 1485 by Lord Henry Clifford, and then restored by Lady Anne Clifford in 1658-59.

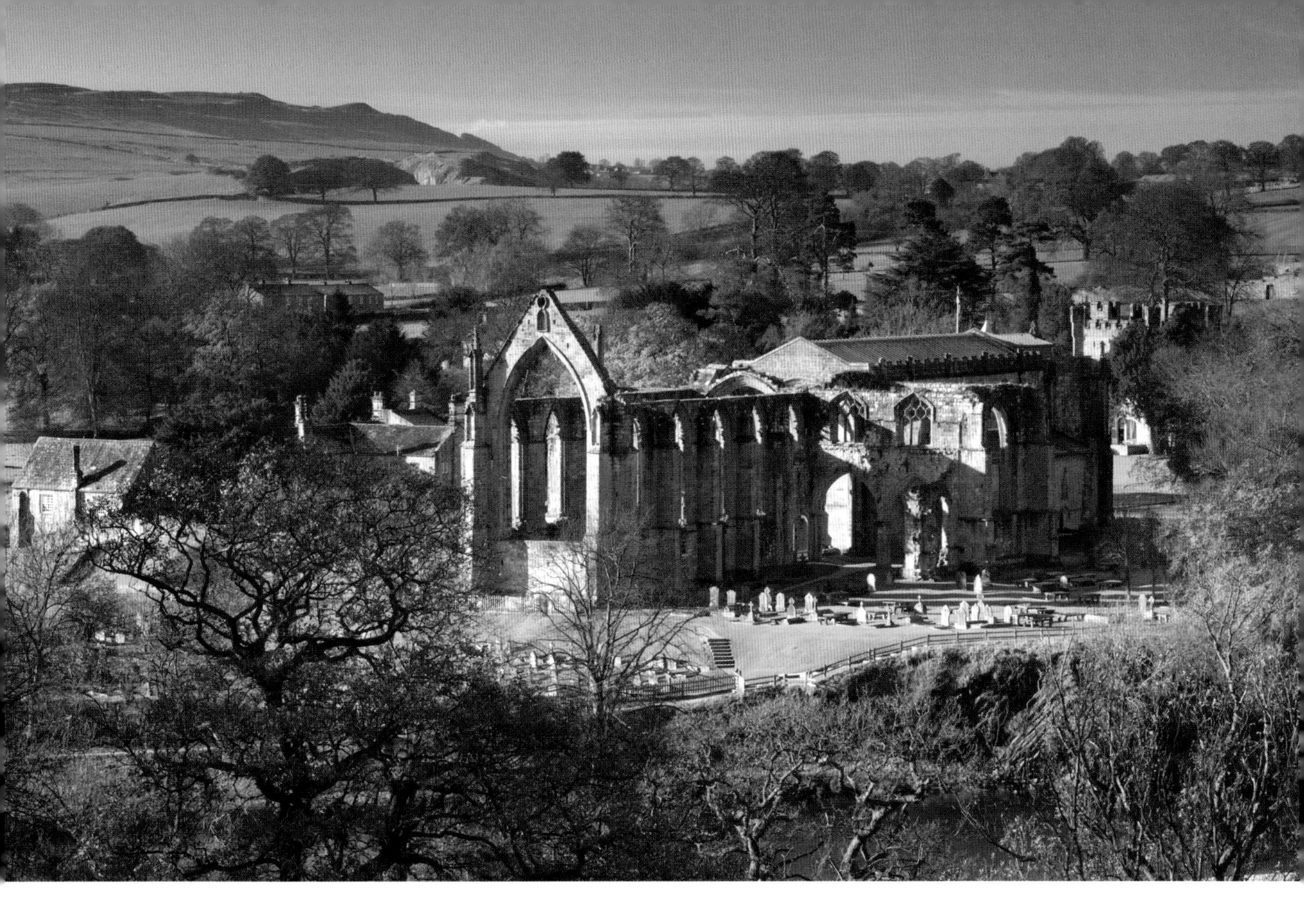

Strid Wood Midway between Bolton Priory and Barden Tower this unique woodland is a Site of Special Scientific Interest because of its rare flora and lichen. The woodland was first opened to the public in 1810 by local rector William Carr who laid out forest paths, one of which leads down to the Strid.

SKIPTON The southern gateway to the Dales, Skipton is situated in Airedale, 22 miles north-west of Leeds. The settlement, which is now a sizeable town, dates from Anglo-Saxon times and is recorded in the Domesday Book as *Sceptone* which means "sheep town". Just a few minutes walk from the hustle and bustle of Skipton's busy high street is this lovely stretch of the Leeds-Liverpool canal (far right), the ideal place for a quiet stroll, or the start of an exploration of the local area on a canal boat. The town has a wide and colourful variety of specialist shops in the ancient courts or "folds" which lead off the high street. In the 1750s Skipton was a thriving centre for the wool trade, and it had its own livestock market. By the end of the century the canal helped bring about the establishment of the worsted cloth industry. Mills began to appear around this time and the town grew rapidly. Between 1650 and 1675 Lady Anne Clifford carried out extensive restoration work to Skipton Castle.

The castle, one of the most complete and well-preserved medieval castles in England, is now privately owned and is open to the public. Its early Tudor courtyard is a great favourite with visitors. Holy Trinity Church has occupied its prominent position at the top of the high street since the early 1100s. Originally constructed in timber it was rebuilt in stone with the help of the monks at Bolton Priory around 1300. Several windows in the church bear the mark of Charles Kempe (1837-1907). Kempe is regarded as one of the giants of Victorian stained-glass craftsmanship.

Gouthwaite Reservoir

The panoramic photograph (right) looks down from Thrope Plantation towards Gouthwaite Reservoir on the river Nidd, a short distance above Pateley Bridge. Constructed in 1899, the road which runs along the side of the reservoir gives access to a nature reserve where there are birdwatching hides for visitors. The area close to the reservoir is a bird-lover's paradise with many birds of prey and a variety of waders. Higher up the river Nidd are Scar House and Angram Reservoirs and to the north-east the reservoirs of Leighton and Roundhill.

MIDDLESMOOR Just seven miles north-west of Pateley Bridge at the head of Nidderdale, Middlesmoor clings to the top of a large hill, its stone cottages and cobbled streets huddled together to form a pretty and interesting hamlet. St Chad's church was restored in 1866 and its set of bells was given by Mrs Barkwith in 1868. The old church was consecrated in 1484 in the reign of Richard III, at the request of the parishioners, by Drummond, Archbishop of York. The font is Anglo Saxon which suggests that there was a church on the site long before the present building. The spectacular view of the vale of Nidd from the churchyard is simply breathtaking. Middlesmoor is an ideal spot for walkers: the Nidderdale Way runs through the village and Scar House Reservoir and Brimham Rocks, with its acres of stunning rock formations, are located close by.

Pateley Bridge The small town of Pateley Bridge has many hidden secrets and should not be overlooked when travelling along the B6265 in upper Nidderdale. Open skies, drystone walls, panoramic views and narrow meandering lanes are all waiting to be discovered on the steep slopes that surround this sheltered settlement. Pateley Bridge's narrow main street is dominated by elegant dark gritstone buildings but on either side there are pretty cobbled alleyways and

passages which lead to hidden and quaint courtyards with a variety of cottages, galleries and craft shops. Over the centuries Pateley Bridge developed as both a market town for the local hill farmers and an industrial centre for both textiles and leadmining. The townsfolk of Pateley Bridge take great pride in their spring and summer floral displays and these have won many awards over the years. The main street has a wide variety of interesting properties including the oldest sweetshop in England (above). This fascinating shop was established in 1827. On the high street there is a plaque marking the start and finish of the Nidderdale Way, a circular route of 53 miles which loops around both sides of the valley.

Ripley Castle This impressive fortified manor house sits on the western edge of the village of Ripley three miles north of Harrogate. The 1,700 acre estate, which includes the village itself, is owned by the Ingilby family who have lived in the castle for over 700 years. The original Tudor castle was transformed into a house in the 1780s; the gatehouse and Old Tower are all that remain of the original castle buildings. The castle saw action during the Civil War; it is still possible to see the impact holes left by musketballs on the courtyard side of the castle resulting from the action of Parliamentary troops. After 1585 it became a treasonable offence to harbour a Catholic priest. The Ingilby family had remained loyal to the Catholic faith and created a priest's hole or hiding place which can be seen on the second floor of the Tower, now known as the knight's chamber.

Brimham Rocks These unique rock formations stand on a hillside four miles east of Pateley Bridge, close to the village of Summerbridge. The rocks are made from millstone grit which has been eroded by wind and water into an amazing collection of weird and wonderful shapes. Some of the rocks have been given imaginative names to match their shapes such as the Sphinx, the Watchdog, the Camel, the Turtle or the Dancing Bear. The rocks stand on a 50 acre site owned by the National Trust.

Uredale

Once the river Ure leaves Wensleydale it continues along Uredale towards Ripon, passing the beautiful abbey at Jervaulx and the villages of Masham and West Tanfield.

Uredale is a prosperous and attractive-farming area and is less rugged than many of the more traditional upland Dales. The pretty towns of Masham and West Tanfield are among its attractions. The riverside city of Ripon with its historic cathedral and attractive canal is an ideal centre for visits to the southern and eastern Dales.

Ripon is also well-situated for trips to the popular Fountains Abbey, Yorkshire's first World Heritage Site – a ruined Cistercian monastery founded in 1132. The abbey ruins are situated within Studley Royal Park, and include one of the best surviving examples of a Georgian water garden in England. The pretty post office (below) is at Boroughbridge, south-east of Ripon.

West Tanfield The village of West Tanfield sits proudly beside the river Ure on the western edge of the Yorkshire Dales, just six miles north of Ripon on the A6108. Crossing the impressive stone bridge over the river, one cannot fail to be moved by the glorious aspect the village has beside the dark meandering waters of the river Ure and the surrounding countryside. Its skyline is dominated by both the Marmion Tower and St Nicholas's church. The medieval parish church stands opposite the Marmion Tower, a 15th-century gatehouse noted for its great arch and oriel window. John Marmion was a knight who died while fighting in Spain under his overlord John of Gaunt, Earl of Richmond. Lady Elizabeth Marmion (neé St Quintin) may have lived in the Marmion Tower after the death of her husband, using it as a "Lady Castle" or Dower House. The tomb (left) commemorating Sir John and Lady Elizabeth Marmion is made from Derbyshire alabaster. Sir John is wearing plate armour typical of the 14th century, and his wife's head rests upon cushions supported by angels.

Fountains Abbey One of the most popular attractions in Yorkshire, Fountains Abbey and Studley Royal is a huge estate which includes the largest abbey ruins in England, a spectacular Georgian water garden and deer park.

MASHAM Pronounced "Massum", this peaceful and attractive small market town is situated midway between Ripon and Leyburn on the A6108. It has many attractions including a generous cobbled market-place surrounded by elegant Georgian houses and stone cottages, shops, galleries, workshops and tea rooms. Other attractions nearby include Jervaulx Abbey and Leighton Reservoir. Masham's reputation amongst the beer-drinking fraternity rests with the famous Black Sheep Brewery, which was established in the early nineties. Its first ales were sampled in 1992. There is a visitor centre at the brewery and tours are very popular indeed.

JERVAULX ABBEY The beautiful ruins of Jervaulx Abbey lie between Masham and Leyburn. The abbey was founded in 1156 by Cistercian monks who moved from Fors, higher up the valley, in search of better weather. The abbey was ruined after the Dissolution of the Monasteries in 1537; much of its fine stonework was looted and used in other local buildings. Despite its condition, enough remains of the ivy-covered crumbling walls to remind the visitor of the simple yet austere lives of the "white monks". A delightful feature of this site today is the large number of wildflowers which decorate the ancient stones and surrounding parkland.

STEAM FAIR
The Masham Steam Engine and Fair Organ rally is a spectacular event which takes place in July. It dates from 1965 and raises funds for the repair and preservation of Masham's impressive town hall which was built in 1913 and used as a convalescent home for troops in WW1. The Masham Sheep Fair takes place each September.

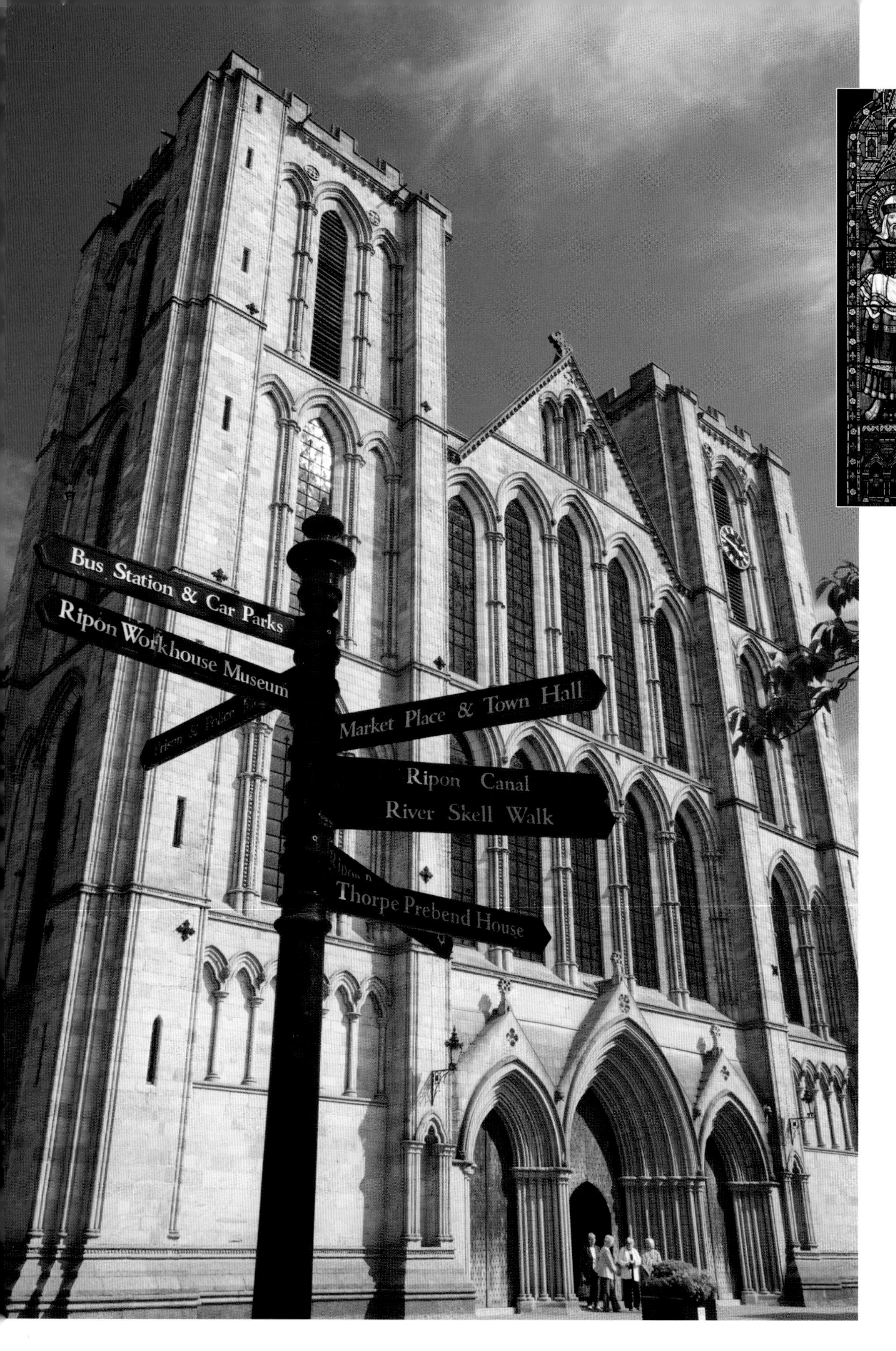

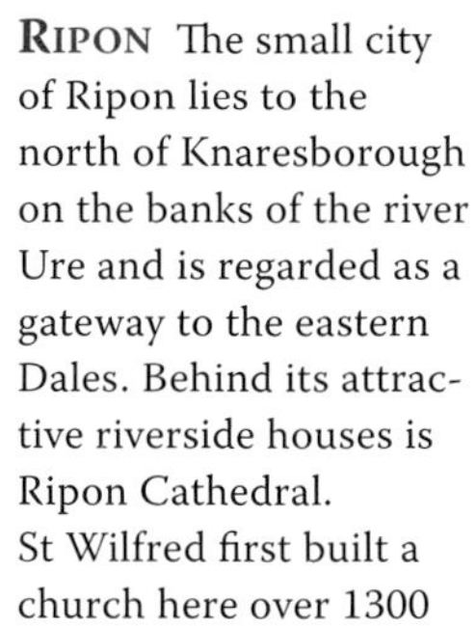

Ripon The small city of Ripon lies to the north of Knaresborough on the banks of the river Ure and is regarded as a gateway to the eastern Dales. Behind its attractive riverside houses is Ripon Cathedral. St Wilfred first built a church here over 1300

years ago but the present building is the fourth on this site. The church did not achieve cathedral status until 1836 when the diocese of Ripon was created. The western front and towers are fine examples of early English church architecture. The Decorated nave (left) dates from the 15th century.

Ripon has three museums – the Courthouse Museum, the Prison and Police Museum and the Workhouse Museum of Poor Law. The Courthouse Museum featured in Yorkshire Television's *Heartbeat*. The canal at Ripon was constructed to connect Ripon to the river Ure at Oxclose Lock and then via the river Ouse to the Humber and the other waterways of Yorkshire. The cut runs for approximately two and a half miles (4km) and has three locks. There is a large marina on the south side of the city close to the racecourse. Fourteen days of flat racing are staged between April and August at Yorkshire's Garden Racecourse each year – in fact, racing has been part of Ripon's life since 1664.

NEWBY HALL Sir Christopher Wren guided the design of Newby Hall (left), near Ripon, built in 1697. Since 1748 it has been home to the Compton family, whose ancestor William Weddell bought the property and enlarged it during the 1760s. The interior was remodelled by a variety of architects, including Robert Adam, and it is an exceptional example of 18th century interior design. The present grounds were laid out in the 1920s, with herbaceous borders and a dramatic broad grass walk leading down to the river Ure. In 2007 Newby Hall was used for the filming of the television adaptation of Jane Austen's novel *Mansfield Park*. Still privately owned, the house and gardens are open to the public from March to September.

First published in 2011 by Myriad Books Limited
35 Bishopsthorpe Road
London SE26 4PA

ISBN 1 84746 390 8

EAN 978 1 84746 390 6

Designed by Jerry Goldie Graphic Design

Printed in China
www.myriadbooks.com